Arsenal Football Quiz

Most Questions That Will Test
Your Knowledge of the Gunners

*(A Collection of Amazing Trivia Quizzes and Fun
Facts for Die-hard Liverpool Fans)*

Thomas Foster

Published By **Kate Sanders**

Thomas Foster

All Rights Reserved

Arsenal Football Quiz: Most Questions That Will Test Your Knowledge of the Gunners (A Collection of Amazing Trivia Quizzes and Fun Facts for Die-hard Liverpool Fans)

ISBN 978-1-7750979-6-9

No part of this guidebook shall be reproduced in any form without permission in writing from the publisher except in the case of brief quotations embodied in critical articles or reviews.

Legal & Disclaimer

The information contained in this book is not designed to replace or take the place of any form of medicine or professional medical advice. The information in this book has been provided for educational & entertainment purposes only.

The information contained in this book has been compiled from sources deemed reliable, and it is accurate to the best of the Author's knowledge; however, the Author cannot guarantee its accuracy and validity and cannot be held liable for any errors or omissions. Changes are periodically made to this book. You must consult your doctor or get professional medical advice before using any of the suggested remedies, techniques, or information in this book.

Upon using the information contained in this book, you agree to hold harmless the Author from and against any damages, costs, and expenses, including any legal fees potentially resulting from the application of any of the information provided by this guide. This disclaimer applies to any damages or injury caused by the use and application, whether directly or indirectly, of any advice or information presented, whether for breach of contract, tort, negligence, personal injury, criminal intent, or under any other cause of action.

You agree to accept all risks of using the information presented inside this book. You need to consult a professional medical practitioner in order to ensure you are both able and healthy enough to participate in this program.

Table Of Contents

Chapter 1: Take Home The Fa Cup 1

Chapter 2: The Time Of Premier League .. 6

Chapter 3: Chapman Managed Directly Before Arsenal 15

Chapter 4: Newcastle During 1998's Cup Final 24

Chapter 5: Player For 6 Seasons In Arsenal Playing 22 Games 30

Chapter 6: The First 1993 Fa Cup Final? . 36

Chapter 7: What Decade Was Don Howe Manage Arsenal 53

Chapter 8: Robert Pires Was Signed Which Arsenal Manager 62

Chapter 9: Who Was Crowned As The Vie-Captain Of 2001? 71

Chapter 10: Origin 84

Chapter 11: Stadium 94

Chapter 12: Managers 105

Chapter 13: Goalies 116

Chapter 14: Defenders 128

Chapter 15: Midfielders 136

Chapter 16: Forwards 147

Chapter 17: Captains 153

Chapter 18: Titles 164

Chapter 19: Memorable Games 174

Chapter 1: Take Home The Fa Cup

Round 1 1. Who was the first to join Arsenal in 1976 after a move from Stoke City?

2. Who was the person who signed with Arsenal in 1999, for PS4.5 millions in 1999? Inter Milan?

3. What was the length of time Robin Van Persie spend at Arsenal?

4. Who was the new Arsenal manager following the unexpected death of Herbert Chapman?

5. Who did you score Arsenals their first Premier League goal in 1992?

6. The number of times Terry Neill win the FA Cup while playing for Arsenal?

7. What was the age of Tony Adams when he was named Arsenal captain?

8. Which Arsenal player received an MBE in 1999's Birthday Honours?

9. Who was sacked twice during the opening three month of his Arsenal time in 2010.

10. Who was the defender who has joined Arsenal in 1987, after having left Wimbledon?

11. Which team did Arsenal beat in 1979's FA Cup Final?

12. Who was knocked out from this year's World cup and 2 months of the 2001-2002 campaign after suffering a cruciate ligament injury?

13. Who resigned from Arsenal in 1988, after having left Stoke City?

14. Who defeated Arsenal at the end of 1979-80's Cup Winners cup?

15. who was Arsenals kit provider from the year the year 1970 to 1986?

16. What titles in the league were Alan Smith win with Arsenal?

17. What year did Arsenal bet the Cup Winners Cup for the first time?

18. What club Did Nigel Winterburn join when he quit Arsenal in the year 2000?

19. The number 5 shirt was worn by who Arsenal player in the 2021-2022 football season?

20. Who was it that Arsenal contract with to purchase PS7.2 million in Mallorca back in the year 2000?

Answers

1. Alan Hudson

2. Kanu

3. 8

4. George Allison

5. Thomas Partey

6. 1

7. 21

8. Tony Adams

9. Laurent Koscielny

10. Nigel Winterburn

11. Manchester United

12. Robert Pires

13. Lee Dixon

14. Valencia

15. Umbro

16. 2

17. 1994

18. Nigel Winterburn

19. Gabriel

20. Lauren

Round 2

1. Arsenal have won their first Fairs Cup for the only occasion in their history with who manager?

2. The last time you scored that was scored for Arsenal was scored in a 2-1 win defeat to

Manchester City at Maine Road in the year 1994?

3. Who scored the most in each round of the Arsenal 1995 Cup Winners Cup campaign?

4. Which city was it that Arsenal defeated Southampton to take home the 2003 FA Cup?

5. Who was the captain of Arsenal during 1971's FA Cup Final?

6. Which player scored the opening strike in the 1971 FA Cup Final for Arsenal during the 1971 FA Cup Final?

7. How many instances did Thierry Henry get an Arsenal Hat Trick for Arsenal in his entire career?

8. Who was the player who scored Arsenal play a 3-2 beta during the 2014 Fa Cup Final?

9. Who did you beat Arsenal during the 1999/2000 UEFA Cup Final?

Chapter 2: The Time Of Premier League
Round 4

1. How many times Bertie Mee managed Arsenal to FA Cup victory?

2. Who resigned from Arsenal in 2006 to move to Portsmouth?

3. Cliff Bastin sine for Arsenal in what year?

4. What was the length of time Jose Reyes spend at Arsenal?

5. What number of shirt did Emmanuel Eboue wear in the 2005-2006 Champions League Final?

6. Who did 12 Hat Tricks in the Arsenal between 1926-1933? Arsenal in 1926-33?

7. What was the age of David O Leary when he made his Arsenal debut?

8. Tony Adams was sent off at least a dozen times throughout the course of his Arsenal career?

9. Who was elected club captain of the club in 1977?

10. Who did you score the goal that opened Arsenal during the 2014 FA Cup Final?

11. What Arsenal player was traded for Crystal Palace in exchange for Peter Nicholas?

12. What was the final score of the 1979 FA Cup Final when Arsenal beat Manchester United?

13. Mohammed Elneny, in the Arsenal team at the beginning of the 2016-2017 football season is of what nationality?

14. In how many instances have Tony Adams win the League cup alongside Arsenal?

15. Who has signed Dennis Bergkamp for Arsenal?

16. What was the sole year in the 1970s which Arsenal were crowned league champions?

17. Who succeeded George Graham as manager of Arsenal?

18. Who were selected for the Fifa World XI in 2006?

19. Which year was it that Steve Bould play his final match for Arsenal?

20. Theo Walcott wore which shirt number with Arsenal during the 2016-2017 football season?

Answers

1. 1

2. Lauren

3. 1929

4. 3

5. 27

6. Jack Lambert

7. 17

8. 4

9. Pat Rice

10. Theo Walcott

11. David Price

12. 3v2

13. Egyptian

14. 2

15. Bruce Rioch

16. 1971

17. Steve Burtenshaw

18. Thierry Henry

19. 1999

20. 14

Round 5

1. How many Englishmen were involved with Arsenal in 1998's FA Cup Final?

2. Which Arsenal player was the second Arsenal player to get sent home during the FA Cup Final?

3. What year did Arsenal take home the League Cup for the first time?

4. Thun from Arsenal's phase group of 2005 and 2006's Champions League, were from Which nation?

5. What was the amount Arsenal pay Marseilles to purchase Robert Pires?

6. In how many occasions did Arsenal be crowned the FA Cup between 2000-2010?

7. Who were sent off during extra time during the 2005 FA Cup Final?

8. Who did you score an unbeaten hat trick during the most famous match ever played at Highbury?

9. What was Arsenals highest scoring player in their debut season in the Premier League?

10. Who has claimed that he had been racially assaulted during a game in 2002 with Lazio during the Urfa Cup?

11. Who was the first to join Arsenal to take on arch-rivals Spurs back in the year 1977?

12. Gabriel is a member of the Arsenal team at the beginning of the season 2016/2017, has what nationality?

13. What year did Thierry Henry quit Arsenal?

14. Who was named as Assistant Manager of Arsenal at the end of 2012?

15. For his 460 appearances at Arsenal which was the percentage of wins for George Graham?

16. Who was the first player to score a score for Arsenal in 1996 during the 2-2 draw against Derby County?

17. Which club was it that Robert Pires join Arsenal in 2000?

18. What team Did Arsenal make an offer to Patrick Viera?

19. What year was the last time JVC begin to offer sponsorship for Arsenals T-shirts?

20. Bruce Rioch was appointed Arsenal manager in what year?

Answers

1. 6

2. Jose Reyes

3. 1987

4. Switzerland

5. PS6 Million

6. 3

7. Reyes

8. Thierry Henry

9. Ian Wright

10. Patrick Viera

11. Willie Young

12. Brazilian

13. 2007

14. Steve Bould

15. 48

16. Patrick Viera

17. Marseille

18. AC Milan

19. 1982

20. 1995

Round 6

1. Who was the first to join Arsenal in 2004 when they were Feyernoord?

2. Who was it that Arsenal to pay Auxerre PS7 million in 2007?

3. Which nationality was the former Arsenal fullback Lauren?

4. Which Arsenal player has the record for having the longest number of appearances in the League Cup (as of 2017)?

5. The date when Pat Rice play his final game with Arsenal?

6. In 2005, when Patrick Viera left Arsenal in 2005, which team did He joined?

7. What did Arsenal end up in the 2013-2014 Premier League?

8. Which Arsenal legend was sentenced to two weeks in Prison in the year 1991?

9. Was the final result at the end of full-time during the final of 2005's Fa Cup Final?

10. Who was the player Arsenal lose to at the time of 1950's FA Cup Final?

11. Who scored a thirty yards strike during 2002's FA Cup Final against Chelsea?

Chapter 3: Chapman Managed Directly Before Arsenal

Round 7

1. The 2003-2004 season was what was the number of games Arsenal draw?

2. Which club Did Mattieu Flamini sign with Arsenal at the end of 2003?

3. Jens Lehman belongs to what country?

4. Who did you score a 119th-minute winner in the 119th minute for Arsenal at the time of 1993's FA Cup Final replay?

5. How many times were Arsenal participate in league play during the 70s?

6. What League titles were Ray Parlour win with Arsenal?

7. The number of times George Graham manager Arsenal to League Cup success?

8. What was the location where 2002's FA Cup Final, won by Arsenal took place?

9. Alex Iwobi, in the Arsenal team at the beginning of the 2016-2017 football season is of what country?

10. Who quit Arsenal in 2016 to be a part of Sparta Prague?

11. Who was the goal scorer for Arsenal during the 2014 FA Cup Final?

12. The 2005-2006 season saw Arsenal established the Champions League record by going for how many matches without conceding goals?

13. Who was the manager of Arsenal between 1962 and 1966?

14. What team did Arsenal lose to at the time of 2003's FA Cup Final?

15. Who was the first to open the Emirates Stadium in 2005?

16. Who was the person who signed Ian Wright for Arsenal?

17. Where was Kanu move to after leaving Arsenal in the year 2004?

18. Who was Robin Van Persie join when Robin Van Persie was released from Arsenal at the end of 2012?

19. Who was the first to join Arsenal in the year 1976, having come from Newcastle United?

20. Who broke the Arsenal records for transfers by more than PS5 million at the time he joined Arsenal club back in the year 1995?

Answers

1. 12

2. Marseille

3. German

4. Andy Linighan

5. 1

6. 3

7. 2

8. Cardiff

9. Nigerian

10. Tomas Roskicky

11. Aaron Ramsey

12. 10

13. Billy Wright

14. Southampton

15. Prince Phillip

16. George Graham

17. West Brom

18. Man Utd

19. Malcolm MacDonald

20. Dennis Bergkamp

Round 8

1. What year was it that Arsenal defeat Aston Villa 4-0 in the FA Cup Final?

2. "One Nil to the Arsenal" was created during what manager's era?

3. Gilles Grimaldi played at Arsenal in what season?

4. What number of other non English players were part of the team of 1971? FA Cup winning Arsenal team?

5. Who was banned for that 1993 League Cup final having been sent off during the semi final win against Spurs?

6. Lucas Perez, , in the Arsenal team at the beginning of the season 2016-2017, is he of what country?

7. Who scored goals for Both Arsenal as well as Spurs in the Premier League North London Derbies?

8. Who was the player loaned to Brighton in the 2016-2017 season?

9. Dennis Bergkamp scored his first goals with Arsenal against what team?

10. Steve Burtnenshaw briefly oversaw Arsenal in the year?

11. Which UEFA Cup Winners Cups did Tony Adams win with Arsenal?0

12. Who was the manager of Arsenal between 1915 and1919?

13. The shirt with the number 2 was worn by whom Arsenal player during the season 2016-2017?

14. Who has scored 228 goals over 377 games at Arsenal?

15. What number of games Did Jose Reyes player for Arsenal?

16. What number of League championships did Arsenal take home in the 1940s?

17. Who was the first player to make his debut with Arsenal during the 2004 game against Manchester United?

18. Who was banned at the time of 2005's Fa cup Final of Arsenal?

19. Who was a player in Oxford, Birmingham and Wimbeldon prior to joining Arsenal in the early 1980s?

20. What percentage of his 416 matches under his charge at Arsenal were they able to win? Terry Neill win?

Answers

1. 2015

2. George Allison

3. 5

4. 3

5. Lee Dixon

6. Spanish

7. Emmanuel Adebayor

8. Chuba Akpom

9. Southampton

10. 1986

11. 1

12. James McEwen

13. Mathieu Debuchy

14. Thierry Henry

15. 69

16. 1

17. Robin Van Persie

18. Jose Reyes

19. Nigel Winterburn

20. 187

Round 9

1. What score was it that Arsenal defeat Newcastle during 1998's Cup Final?

2. Which player scored the sole goal in Arsenals Semi Final in 2005-2006 of the 2005 and 2006 Champions League, the year when they were in the final?

3. Who began his career with Arsenal in 1984, then left in 1986, and then returned in 1993?

4. Which player did Arsenal beat in an Replay in order to take in 1993 the FA cup?

5. What is Ian Wright's middle name?

6. What's the proper name for Arsenal?

7. Cliff Bastin actually played in which the position?

8. Which club was the team that Paul Merson join after he quit Arsenal at the end of 1997?

9. Which player did Arsenal lose 2-1 to at the time of 1993's FA Cup Final Replay?

10. What year was the year that Robin Van Persie leave Arsenal?

20. Arsene Wenger

Chapter 4: Newcastle During 1998's Cup Final

Round 10

1. Who was crowned in 2006 the Rotterdam Sportsman of the Year?

2. Who took the penalty goal in Arsenals famed 2009 Champions League win over Roma?

3. Who was elected club captain of the club in 1983?

4. Who served two times as Arsenal manager on either side of Bruch Rioch's time?

5. In how many instances did Arsenal have the honour of winning the FA Cup in the 1970s?

6. Who recorded 108 goals in 300 matches with Arsenal?

7. What was the score when Arsenal beat Manchester United on penalties in the 2005 FA Cup?

8. Who was the player Arsenal defeat 1-0 in the 2003 FA Cup Semi Final?

9. Who was the person who signed Pat Jennings for Arsenal?

10. Which year was the year that Arsenal participate for the first time in an FA Cup Final for the first time?

11. How many Englishman began their career in 1999-2000? UEFA Cup Final for Arsenal?

12. In the years 2016 and 2017 who was the vice-captain of Arsenal?

13. Davor Suker , a former Arsenal player, has what country of origin?

14. Kanu has spent what number of seasons at Arsenal?

15. Who was the player who was loaned to Roma in the 2016-2017 football season?

16. Who crashed into his Ford Sierra and was found to be drunk driving in the year 1990?

17. Since 2017 what is the most number of times Arsenal participated during the Champions League final?

18. What was the number of times Arsenal take home the FA Cup in the 1990s?

19. What was the number of times Thierry Henry take home the European Golden Boot at Arsenal?

20. What year was it that Arsenal take home their FA Cup Final on penalties?

Answers

1. Robin Van Persie

2. Robin Van Persie

3. Graham Rix

4. Stewart Houston

5. 2

6. Frank Stapleton

7. 5v4

8. Sheffield United

9. Terry Neill

10. 1927

11. 5

12. Laurent Koscielny

13. Croatia

14. 5

15. Wojciech Szczensy

16. Tony Adams

17. 1

18. 2

19. 3

20. 2005

Round 11

1. Who scored two goals at the time of the 1950 FA Cup Final for Arsenal?

2. In 2012, when he joined Arsenal back in the year 2012 which number of shirt was Lukas the Podolski handed?

3. Who succeeded Bertie Mee as Arsenal Manager?

4. Danny Welbeck wore which shirt number at Arsenal during the 2016-2017 Arsenal season?

5. When did Freddie Ljunberg leave Arsenal?

6. Terry Neill managed Arsenal for the length of time?

7. Who did you score the winner's goal during the 1979 FA Cup Final?

8. Who was the scorer with Arsenal during the 1982 FA Cup Final?

9. Who was the first to join Arsenal in 1977 after leaving Wolves?

10. Who was the player that Arsenal select for Lorient in the year 2010?

11. Was the final result at the end of full-time during the final of 2005's FA Cup Final?

12. Which team did Arsenal get to in the initial season in the Premier League?

13. When did Lauren sign for Arsenal?

14. Patrick Viera was sent off several times during the course of his Arsenal career?

15. Who was a player for 6 seasons in Arsenal playing 22 games?

16. Which Arsenal player quit from the club to join the club in 2008. He returned to the club in?

17. Who was the player hired by Arsenal in 1995 after leaving Sampdoria?

18. Robert Pires, the former Arsenal player, has what country of origin?

Chapter 5: Player For 6 Seasons In Arsenal Playing 22 Games

Round 12

1. Yaya Sanogo has been signed by which club?

2. Who was as the FWA footballer of the year in 2002?

3. Who did you score the winner's goal during the 2003 FA Cup final against Southampton?

4. Who was the first to join Arsenal in 1995, after having left Inter Milan?

5. Who was the team that Arsenal defeated 1-0 in Final of 2003's FA Cup?

6. The year of the appointment Bertie Mee appointed as Arsenal Manager?

7. Who was the person Arsenal select to receive PS450,000 in 1979? Ipswich from 1979?

8. Who finished as runner-up in 2003's Fifa World Player of the Year Award?

9. What Arsenal footballer was the very first foreigner to receive the PFA Player of the Year Award?

10. Who was the captain who led Arsenal to victory at 1987's League Cup Final in 1987?

11. Who played in the 458 matches with Arsenal between the years 1988-2002?

12. What was the age of Cesc Fabregas when he was the youngest player at Arsenal?

13. Bruce Rioch was sacked from Arsenal for poor performances. What was his percentage of success?

14. What was the number of times during the 90s did Arsenal take home the FA Cup/League Cup?

15. Who was the 1999 winner of the FA Cup? Arsenal lose to win the FA Cup?

16. Kolo Toure was a player for what years with Arsenal?

17. Robin Van Persie scored how many goals in the Premier League against Spurs during the Premier League?

18. Who made Arsenals shirt between the 1930s and the 1970s?

19. Who did Cliff Bastin's Arsenal record for scoring in 1997?

20. What was the number of times Lee Dixon win the FA Cup while playing for Arsenal?

Answers

1. Auxerre

2. Robert Pires

3. Robert Pires

4. Dennis Bergkamp

5. Southampton

6. 1966

7. Brian Talbot

8. Thierry Henry

9. Liam Brady

10. Kenny Samson

11. Lee Dixon

12. 16

13. 46%

14. 2

15. Newcastle United

16. 7

17. 5

18. Bukta

19. Ian Wright

20. 3

Round 13

1. 1. Who has been "wrongfully dismissed" in a match in 2015 against Chelsea?

2. Who scored the first goal with Arsenal in the second match against Liverpool in the year 2000?

3. Who was the Telegraph identify as "21 going on 9" following a wild tackle on Graeme Le Saux?

4. Giles Grimaldi was sent off numerous times throughout the course of his Arsenal career?

Five. Who ranks 1st on the Arsenal.com listing for"the Gunners 50 Greatest Players?

6. Who scored his Arsenal debut with a 3-0 win against Man United in 1998?

7. What shade of shirt were Arsenal wearing during 1979's FA Cup Final?

8. What year was it that Robin Van Persie join Arsenal?

9. Who made 64 appearances in the Premier League for Arsenal during 7 years with 4 goals, and scoring four before 2010.

10. The year was when Tony Adams make his Arsenal debut?

11. What year when did Patrick Viera become club captain at Arsenal?

12. Who was the manager of Arsenal during four matches before the arrival Arsene Wenger?

13. Arsenal was the first to win this FA Cup in what year?

14. Granit Xhaka , who was in the Arsenal team at the beginning of the season 2016-2017, is he of which nationality?

Chapter 6: The First 1993 Fa Cup Final?
Round 15

1. What year was it that Arsenal Wenger take over as Arsenal manager?

2. Davor Suker was a member of Arsenal in which year?

3. Ian Wright scored a hat goal on his debut league game for Arsenal against who?

4. Patrick Viera joined Arsenal in what year?

5. Who did you score the second goal in the 69th minutes of the 1998 FA Cup Final?

6. Who scored record seven goals for Arsenal in a league game in a match against Aston Villa?

7. Who played 558 times with Arsenal between the year 1975 and 1993?

8. Sylvain Wiltord quit Arsenal in what year?

9. Which manager is Arsenal the second manager with the longest tenure?

10. Who hit a 30-yard blaster that gave Arsenal an 2-1 victory over Valencia during the 2002 champions League quarter final?

11. Prior to the victory in the title race of 2004 How many titles in the league were Arsenal been awarded?

12. How many Northern Irish men managed Arsenal during the latter 20th Century?

13. Who was the leader of in the Premier League assists chart for the season 2001-2002?

14. From what club Did Arsenal make an offer to Tomas Rossklciy?

15. What's the capacity of the Emirate stadium as of 2016, and what is the capacity of the Emirate stadium?

16. Who has scored 29 goals in 279 matches with Arsenal?

17. Which footballer did Arsenal lend for Watford during 2014?

18. Patrick Viera scored how many goals in the Premier League against Spurs during the Premier League?

19. The date when Steve Bould make his Arsenal debut?

20. The date when did Lauren take part in his last game at Arsenal?

Answers

1. 1996

2. 1999

3. Southampton

4. 1996

5. Nicola Anelka

6. Ted Drake

7. David O Leary

8. 2004

9. George Allison

10. Ray Parlour

11. 13

12. 2

13. Robert Pires

14. Borussia Dortmund

15. 60,432

16. Patrick Viera

17. Hector Bellerin

18. 4

19. 1988

20. 2006

Round 16

1. Who was the first to join Arsenal in 2002, after having left ASEC Mimosas?

2. Where was Freddie Ljunberg go when he quit Arsenal back in the year 2007?

3. The date when Robert Pires play his final match for Arsenal?

4. Which was the sole player who scored for Arsenal in the year 2000 UEFA Cup Final penalty shootout?

5. To and including Stewart Houston, how many Scotsmen have been in charge of Arsenal?

6. Who was the player Arsenal lose to during the 1936 FA Cup Final?

7. Who was referred to by the name of "the Romford Pele"?

8. What was the amount Arsenal spend on Crystal Palace for Ian Wright in the year 1991?

9. Who scored an incredible third goal to Arsenal in their 2 - 0 FA Cup final win over Chelsea in 2002?

10. Who was the player Arsenal take on to draw an 0-0 draw during the 2005 FA Cup Final?

11. George Graham signed which of the following players with Arsenal back in 1987?

12. What was the average time Arsenal complete"Double" "Double" in the 20th century?

13. How many league championships did Arsenal get during the 1940s?

14. What time was the last time Ray Parlour make his last appearance at Arsenal?

15. In 2004, who won the FWA Footballer of the Year?

16. Per Mertesacker signed for Arsenal in what year?

17. What city Did Arsenal take part in the final match of the 1994-1995 Urfa Cup Winners Cup?

18. Who did 12 hat-tricks for Arsenal between 1921 and 1931?

19. The shirt with the number 11 was worn by whom Arsenal player during the season 2016-2017?

20. The year was when David Seaman make his first Arsenal appearance?

Answers

1. Kolo Toure

2. West Ham United

3. 2006

4. Ray Parlour

5. 5

6. Sheffield United

7. Ray Parlour

8. PS2.5 million

9. Freddie Ljunberg

10. Man Utd

11. Nigel Winterburn

12. 2

13. 1

14. 2007

15. Thierry Henry

16. 2011

17. Paris

18. Jim Brain

19. Mesut Ozil

20. 1990

Round 17

1. Who was the captain of Arsenal during the 1979 FA Cup Final?

2. Which footballer was signed by Arsenal in 2006 before leaving in the year 2016?

3. Which player was league's most prolific overall scorer in the season 1988-1989?

4. Who ran Arsenal during the 10 years that ran between 1966 to 1976?

5. Berite Mee quit Arsenal in what year?

6. What number of First Division titles did Herbert Chapman get during his time at Arsenal?

7. William was the actual initial name for the former Arsenal manager?

8. Who started to provide Arsenals with their football shirts in 2014?

9. What team did Arsenal beat during the 2003 FA Cup Semi Final?

10. Who was the player loaned to Bournemouth during the season 2016-2017?

11. What year did George Graham leave Arsenal as manager?

12. What is the nationality of ex- Arsenal footballer Bacary Sagna?

13. In how many instances were there George Graham win the Charity Shield in his capacity as Arsenal manager?

14. Who was named as the PFA Premier League Team of the Year in 1996, 1994 and 1997 playing for Arsenal?

15. What year did Alan Smith play his final match for Arsenal?

16. Who was the first to join Arsenal 1999 after leaving Dynamo Kiev?

17. The date on which George Swindon leave his post as Arsenal manager?

18. Who took Arsenal towards their very first FA Cup?

19. Who was exiled twice within 72 hours of the first game of the 2001-2001 campaign?

20. Who was given a loan the club Sporting CP for the 2016-2017 season?

Answers

1. Pat Rice

2. Tomas Roskicky

3. Alan Smith

4. Bertie Mee

5. 1976

6. 2

7. Terry Neill

8. Puma

9. Sheffield United

10. Jack Wilshere

11. 1995

12. French

13. 1

14. Tony Adams

15. 1995

16. Luzhny

17. 1962

18. Herbert Chapman

19. Patrick Viera

20. Joel Campbell

Round 18

1. What city was it that in 2006 the Champions League final take place?

2. Which Arsenal manager suddenly passed away from Pnuemonia at the age of 55?

3. All in all, how numerous occasions did Slyvinho have a stint with Arsenal?

4. How many instances did Terry Neil manage Arsenal during the European Cup Final?

5. Who won the FWA Footballer of the Year in 2003?

6. Who has joined Arsenal in the year 2000, having come from Marseille?

7. What time did David O Leary play his last Arsenal match?

8. Who was the one to score the second goal of Arsenals two goals during 1999's FA Cup Final?

9. Who was the person Arsenal choose to sign 2012 with after acquiring FC Koln?

10. Who has scored the most goals the most goals for Arsenal the most often during the Champions League as of 2016?

11. Which team did Arsenal end up during 2015 and 2016? Premier League Season?

12. In how many matches Did Bertie Mee take charge if Arsenal?

13. Tom Whittaker was in charge of Arsenal for what number of years?

14. Who was the first to join Arsenal in 1990 for PS1.3 million back in the year 1990? QPR?

15. Who made a famous two-finger salute after scoring for Arsenal?

16. What was the result in the final? Arsenal defeated Parma in the 1994 Cup Winners Cup Final?

17. What was the very first manager at Arsenal?

18. Who was the team that Arsenal defeat 2-1 in Semi-Finals in 1979-80 Cup Winners Cup?

19. Who led Arsenal towards victory during 1950's FA Cup Final?

Answers

1. Paris

2. Herbert Chapman

3.

4. 80

5. 1

6. Thierry Henry

7. Robert Pires

8. 1993

9. Nicolas Anelka

10. Lukas Podolski

11. Thierry Henry

12. 2nd

13. 539

14. 9

15. David Seaman

16. Kanu

17. 1v0

18. Thomas Mitchell

19. Juventus

20. Joe Mercer

Round 19

1. Was the final score of Arsenal won against Chelsea in 2002's FA Cup Final?

2. Lee Dixon won how many League titles at Arsenal?

3. Who took over from Billy Wright as manager of Arsenal?

4. In which minute did Nayim get the win at the end of the 1995-1994 Urfa Cup Winners Cup?

5. What league titles did Tony Adams win with Arsenal?

6. What year did Arsenal become the first team to be awarded the FA Cup/League Cup twice?

7. What team did Arsenal acquire David Seaman from in 1990?

8. The date when David Seaman play his final match for Arsenal?

9. Slyvinho who was a ex- Arsenal player, has what is his nationality?

10. What if he said he would not wish to play during a 2006. Champions League match against NK Dimano Zagreb to ensure he would not get cup-toed in the possibility of a transfer?

11. What was the one Arsenal player to be named as a player in 2015's PFA Team of the Year?

12. Which player was fined a total of PS45,000 and was banned for six games in 1999/200?

13. Who was the Arsenal Manager who was Northern Irish?

14. Who was it that Liverpool lose to on the final day of football to claim the league title in 1989?

15. What Premier League team did Lauren sign up to after leaving Arsenal?

16. Which Arsenal player won the title of Man of the Match at the 1999 FA Cup Final?

17. What decade was Don Howe manage Arsenal?

Chapter 7: What Decade Was Don Howe Manage Arsenal

Round 21

1. How long were Billy Wright in charge of Arsenal?

2. Which player was Arsenals highest scorer both in the 1981-1982 and 1979-1980 seasons?

3. Who scored six goals in the Premier League for Arsenal in the very first Season in the Premier League?

4. What were your opposition for the game that was played at the Emirates?

5. Was the final score during 1999 and 2000? UEFA Cup Final?

6. In how many occasions did Arsenal take home the FA Cup in the 1950s?

7. In what decade in which decade did Arsenal have five League titles?

8. Which country is Arsenal footballer Yaya Sanogo?

9. Which footballer left Arsenal in 2009 in order to move to Manchester City?

10. What was the number of times Robert Pires score against Spurs in the Premier League?

11. What was the result what was the final score Arsenal were beaten by Liverpool during the 1950 FA Cup Final?

12. In which year did Bruce Rioch sacked from his job in the role of Arsenal manager?

13. Who took home the PFA Players Player of the Year Award in 1998, while playing for Arsenal?

14. Who was the 2003 PFA Award-winning Player?

15. Who has scored the 100th goal of his career for Arsenal during a match between 2000 and 2003 in the match against Oxford United?

16. The year was when Arsenal first take home this award? FA Charity Shield?

17. Jack Crayston was manager of Arsenal during what period?

18. Who was the first to join Arsenal in 1999 after leaving Juventus?

19. Which non-league team did Arsenal lose 5-1 to in the fourth round of the 2003 FA Cup?

20. Who made the Arsenal lend money to Leyton Orent in 1989?

Answers

1. 4

2. Alan Sunderland

3. Paul Merson

4. Ajax

5. 0v0

6. 1

7. 1930s

8. French

9. Kolo Toure

10. 7

11. 2v0

12. 1996

13. Dennis Bergkamp

14. Thierry Henry

15. Dennis Bergkamp

16. 1930

17. 1950s

18. Thierry Henry

19. Farnborough Town

20. Kevin Campbell

Round 22

1. In the beginning of the season 2016-2017, who among these players has been with Arsenal for the longest time?

2. The number 8 shirt was worn by who Arsenal player during the season 2016-2017?

3. Who did Arsenal score the winning goal during the 2003 FA Cup Final win over Southampton?

4. Arsenal has signed which of these players of Auxerre?

5. In the two years he spent during his time at Arsenal, Stefan Malz made what number of appearances?

6. Who did you score a hat-trick in the 4-2 victory over Werder Bremen in a UEFA cup Quarter-Final in 2000?

7. Who scored the winning goal during the Semi Final 2nd Leg in the 2000 UEFA CUP against Lens?

8. What was Arsenals highest scorer during four consecutive seasons in the 80s?

9. With whom did Steve Bould score Arsenal's first ever Premier League goal in 1992?

10. Don Howe was sacked as manager of Arsenal in which year?

11. Arsenal has signed Ian Wright from which club?

12. In the year Robert Pires left Arsenal, the club he signed him to was Spanish club?

13. who was sent to the side during a 1998 Fa cup quarterfinal due to pushing Steve Lomas?

14. How long ago did Arsenal became the first London team to play in the Champions League Final?

15. Who was the person Arsenal choose to sign with Real Madrid in 2013?

16. Which of the games was sponsored by company Arsenals shirt between 1999 and 2002?

17. How much did Arsenal pay Inter Milan for Dennis Bergkamp?

18. who admitted having issues with gambling and cocaine in 1994?

19. Which club Did Robin Van Persie join Arsenal?

20. Which First Division titles did George Graham get while at Arsenal?

Answers

1. Theo Walcott

2. Aaron Ramsey

3. Robert Pires

4. Yaya Sanogo

5. 6

6. Ray Parlour

7. Kanu

8. Alan Smith

9. Norwich City

10. 1986

11. Crystal Palace

12. Villarreal

13. Dennis Bergkamp

14. 2006

15. Mesuit Ozil

16. Sega

17. PS7.5 Million

18. Paul Merson

19. Feyenoord

20. 2

Round 23

1. Who was the man of the match at 2015? FA Cup Final?

2. Who was the player who crossed the ball to win Alan Sunderland winner in the 1979 cup final?

3. Ian Wright scored how many goals in the Premier League against Spurs within the Premier League?

4. Which player scored the winning goal that won in the year 70th Fairs Cup for Arsenal?

5. Who scored the famous double during a game against Manchester United in a 1991 First Division clash?

6. Who was dismissed during the match on Stamford Bridge with Chelsea, after a reckless tackle on Diego Costa?

7. What team was it that Arsenal defeat 4-3 in the Aggregate to take home the 1970 Fairs Cup?

8. Who has scored the goal that Wenger described as "The goal of a lifetime" during a game in 2006 against Charlton?

Chapter 8: Robert Pires Was Signed Which Arsenal Manager

1. What year was it that Arsenal not lose during the Premier League?

2. Which year did Arsene Wenger appointed Arsenal manager?

3. How many times were Terry Neill in charge of Arsenal?

4. Which city was it that Arsenal triumph in their 1995 Cup Winners Cup Final?

5. Which player scored the 2nd of Arsenals goals in 2002's FA Cup Final?

6. Arsenal was awarded the title of league champion several times during the 70s?

7. Who is the Arsenal record for longest number of games for the FA cup (as in the year 2017)?

8. Who was captain of Arsenal for the last time in final match of 1979-1980's Cup Winners Cup?

9. What was the opening goal for Arsenal during the 2014 FA Cup Final?

10. What percentage of points did Arsenal beat Chelsea in 2004 to claim the League Title?

11. What is the nationality of Arsene Wenger?

12. Who was the first to score his most infamous, hat-trick with Arsenal in the match against Leicester City in 1997?

13. What was the result of the final match in the 1993-1994 Cup Winners Cup?

14. For the ten years he was Manager, just how many trophy wins were won by Bertie Mee at Arsenal?

15. What was the price Arsenal pay to purchase Patrick Viera?

16. Who was dismissed for the first occasion in his career during the 1997 match against Sunderland?

17. Which Arsenal player won the vote as 2002's FA Cup Final Man of the Game?

18. Who was the boss of Arsenal in 1934 when they took home in 1934 the First Division Championship?

19. Who left Arsenal in 1978 and joined the Seattle Sounders?

20. Who was crowned as the vie-captain of 2001?

Answers

1. 2003-2004

2. 1996

3. 416

4. Copenhagen

5. Fredrick Ljungberg

6. 1

7. David O Leary

8. Pat Rice

9. Santi Carzola

10. 11

11. French

12. Dennis Bergkamp

13. 1v0

14. 3

15. PS3.5 million

16. Dennis Bergkamp

17. Fredrick Ljungberg

18. Joe Shaw

19. Alan Hudson

20. Patrick Viera

Round 25

1. Phillipe Senderos was sent off several times during the course of his Arsenal career?

2. Which player quit in 1999 arsenal for Nottingham Forest?

3. Arsenal is located on the city in which English city?

4. Who was the Arsenal player who scored in the 2005 Champions League final?

5. Which Arsenal player was famous for his anxiety about flying?

6. Which year was it that Arsenal claim their 6th FA Cup?

7. What penalties did Arsenal miss during the 2005 FA Cup Final?

8. Which player was Arsenals most prolific scorer of the 1978, 1979, and the season of 1980?

9. In 2016, how often did Arsenal been ranked below 14th place in the top league in English football?

10. Anders Limpar was signed by who manager at Arsenal?

11. Petr Cech wore what number of shirt for Arsenal in the 2016-2017 campaign?

12. Who quit Arsenal in the year 1996 to join Manchester City after playing only 22 times?

13. Was the final score in 2006? Barcelona won against Arsenal in 2006's Champions League final?

14. In the 1950s, how numerous occasions did Arsenal won the league?

15. What period was the decade that Billy Wright manage Arsenal?

16. What team did Arsenal lose 2-1 to lift the League Cup for the first time?

17. Which footballer scored 11 of the Hat-tricks for Arsenal between the years 1991-98?

18. Who steered Arsenal until their 1980 European Cup Final?

19. Who was the first to join Arsenal in 1987 after leaving Leicester City?

20. Who defeated Arsenal 4-2 in their debut ever game within the Premier League in 1992?

Answers

1. 3

2. David Platt

3. London

4. Sol Campbell

5. Dennis Bergkamp

6. 1993

7. 0

8. Frank Stapleton

9. 6

10. George Graham

11. 33

12. Paul Dickov

13. 2v1

14. 1

15. 1960s

16. Liverpool

17. Thierry Henry

18. Terry Neill

19. Alan Smith

20. Norwich City

Round 26

1. The number of times Sylvain Wiltord be the winner of the Premier League with Arsenal?

2. Tommy Caton was which managers most recently signing with Arsenal?

3. What was the length of time Ray Parlour spend at Arsenal?

4. Which was Arsenals most popular player for his first season of 1981?

5. Who was the captain for the Arsenal team which took home in 1994 the Cup Winners Cup?

6. Who won the 2004 PFA Players Player of the Year?

7. What championships Did Cliff Bastin win for Arsenal?

8. Who did Arsenal score the goal that led to the draw 1-1 in the 1993 FA Cup Final?

9. Who was the team that Arsenal beat 6-2 in the quarter-final stage of the 1999/2000 UEFA Cup ?

10. What number of Fa Cup titles did Martin Keown take home while playing for Arsenal?

11. Who did Arsenal score the winning goal in 1936's FA Cup Final?

12. Nayim scored a cult 45 yard strike against Arsenal...who was on the goal?

13. Who was the one toe that splintered in 2006 during an FA Cup tie against Cardiff?

14. Total, how many prizes were Herbert Chapman win with Arsenal?

Chapter 9: Who Was Crowned As The Vie-Captain Of 2001?

Round 27

1. How many Englishmen made up the Arsenal team which kicked off at the 2003 FA Cup Final?

2. Who has the record in terms of most Arsenal consecutive appearances, with 172?

3. Which player quit Arsenal in 2014 to join Manchester City?

4. Who was the manager of Arsenal for 9 years starting in 1947?

5. Who did you score a hat-trick in the 6-0 victory over Portsmouth in 1987 at Highbury back in 1987?

6. Phillip Senderos , the former Arsenal player, has what country of origin?

7. Who signed who in 2016 by Borussia Dortmund?

8. Who was the person who scored 11 Hat Tricks at Arsenal between 1934 and 1945?

9. What year was it that Arsenal be the first to win in the FA Cup/League double for the first time?

10. What team did Arsenal beat 2-1 during the 1993 League Cup Final?

11. Francis Coquelin wore which shirt number at Arsenal during the 2016-2017 football season?

12. What is the nationalist of the former Arsenal defensive player Emmanuel Eboue?

13. What team did Arsenal lose 2-1 to during the 1971 FA Cup Final?

14. What was the final score of the 2014 FA Cup Final when Arsenal were able to defeat Hull City?

15. What was the length of time Stefan Schwarz work at Arsenal?

16. In 2016, what number of players had scored more goals at Arsenal over Cliff Bastin?

17. Who was the manager at Arsenal prior to Bertie Mee?

18. In how many occasions did Arsenal be crowned champions of the league during the 1930s?

19. What League titles did Tony Adams win in the 90s?

20. What year did Don Howe appointed as manager of Arsenal?

Answers

1. 4

2. Tom Parker

3. Bacary Sagna

4. Tom Whitaker

5. Alan Smith

6. Swiss

7. Tomas Roskicky

8. Ted Drake

9. 1971

10. Sheffield Wednesday

11. 34

12. Ivorian

13. Liverpool

14. 3v2

15. 1

16. 3

17. Billy Wright

18. 5

19. 2

20. 1983

Round 28

1. Was the final score in Arsenal Beta Huddersfield Town to win the FA Cup for the first time?

2. What player did Arsenal choose to sign with Newcastle during 2014?

3. Who was in charge of Spurs directly BEFORE being in charge of Arsenal?

4. Who was the one who scored for Arsenal in 2002's FA Cup Final win over Chelsea?

5. Total, how many awards have George Graham win with Arsenal?

6. What was Arsenals initial name at the time of its creation?

7. Who was the captain of arsenal during their loss in the 1980 and 1978 cup finals?

8. What did Pat Rice's win percentage in his role as manager at Arsenal?

9. Who was it that Arsenal beat in the semi-final in the 2002 FA Cup?

10. The 504 times he played in the club of Arsenal How many scores Did Tony Adams score?

11. Who was the team that Arsenal defeat 3-1 in the Semi-Finals of the 1999/2000 UEFA Cup?

12. Who was the man who won the the 2014 FA Cup Final?

13. Who quit Arsenal when they joined Athletic Madrid?

14. Who is the player who holds the record for the most EUROPEAN appearances at Arsenal?

15. The winner of the 2006 FWA Footballer of the Year award three times?

16. Who was named The 1989 PFA Young Player of the Year?

17. What club was it that Graham Rix join on leaving Arsenal in 1988?

18. Theo Walcott was signed which Arsenal manager?

19. What decade Did Arsenal have a hard time winning an award for league play?

20. Who was a member of Arsenal with the baffling fee of PS333,333.34?

Answers

1. 2v0

2. Mathieu Debuchy

3. Terry Neill

4. Ray Parlour

5. 7

6. Dial Square

7. Pat Rice

8. 75%

9. Chelsea

10. 32

11. Lens

12. Aaron Ramsey

13. Jose Reyes

14. Thierry Henry

15. Thierry Henry

16. Paul Merson

17. Caen

18. Arsene Wenger

19. 1960s

20. Malcolm MacDonald

Round 29

1. What was the number of times David Seaman win the FA Cup while playing for Arsenal?

2. Who captains Arsenal during the 1980 FA Cup Final?

3. How many awards Did Billy Wright win as Arsenal Manager?

4. Who was the winner of the European Golden Boot twice in consecutive years while playing at Arsenal?

5. Who received an Arsenal number 9 shirt from Arsenal during 2012?

6. How many awards were there? Bruce Rioch win as Arsenal manager?

7. What number of League championships did Arsenal during the 1950s?

8. Who was the manager of Arsenal between 1937 and the year 1947?

9. A statue in honor of who was unveiled in the Emirates in 2011.

10. What was the age of Jock Rutherford was when was the most senior player to play with Arsenal?

11. In how many occasions did Arsenal take home the League title in the 1930s?

12. Mathieu Flamini first joined Arsenal in what year?

13. Who did you think scored 9 in hat-tricks with Arsenal from 1999 to 2012?

14. Who was the first player to make their debut as a player for Arsenal in the 1983 match against Sunderland?

15. Who did you score the goal that opened the FA Cup Final in 1998?

16. Who was the player who made it to Arsenal from 1992 to 2004?

17. Who was captain of Arsenal over 14 years?

18. Who took over from George Swindon as manager of Arsenal?

19. Who was signed by Arsenal in 2000 for the club record PS13 million in the year 2000?

20. What was the nickname Cliff Bastin earn at Arsenal?

Answers

1. 3

2. Pat Rice

3. 0

4. Thierry Henry

5. Lukas Podolski

6. 0

7. 1

8. George Allison

9. Tony Adams

10. 41

11. 5

12. 2004

13. Doug Lishman

14. Tony Adams

15. Marc Overmars

16. Ray Parlour

17. Tony Adams

18. Billy Wright

19. Sylvain Wiltord

20. Boy

Round 30

1. Which England caps have Steve Bould win?

2. What was the number of times Tony Adams lift the FA Cup during the 90s?

3. Who steered Arsenal to win three consecutive FA cups from the 1970s to 1980s?

4. Which Arsenal player left to become a member of Crystal Palace in 2016?

5. Who was the one to concede an offside penalty in his Arsenal debut in 1992 against Liverpool on the pitch in 1992?

6. What was the result of eh 2014. FA Cup Final when Arsenal defeated Hull?

7. What number of performances Did Paul Merson make for Arsenal?

8. Who was the player who did Arsenal choose to sign with Marseille in the year 2004?

9. Clive Allen went in exchange at the time Arsenal who?

10. Who was the captain of Arsenal in 1979's FA Cup Final?

11. What was the price Arsenal have to pay Feyernoord Robin Van Persie?

12. In 2003, David Seaman left Arsenal in 2003 What club did he sign with?

13. In addition to Arsene Wenger How many other men are in charge at Arsenal?

14. Emmanuel Petit was signed which Arsenal manager?

15. Which Arsenal manager was also the first to make a comment about the Derby?

Chapter 10: Origin

20 Trivia Questions

1. In what year was the very first time Arsenal played in the premier division?

A. 1893

B. 1913

C. 1904

D. 1899

2. What was the one and last year that Arsenal was dropped from the league?

A. 1912

B. 1913

C. 1914

D. 1915

3. What year was the Arsenal was founded?

A. 1881

B. 1886

C. 1891

D. 1896

4. Which is the Arsenal's most well-known nicknames?

A. The Reds

B. The Arsenal

C. The Cannons

D. The Gunners

5. Who was the first Arsenal captain?

A. Morris Bates

B. William Stewart

C. David Danskin

D. Arthur Brown

6. The year in which the present Arsenal Crest first was first introduced?

A. 2004

B. 2002

C. 2000

D. 1998

7. What year did Arsenal become a member of in the English Football League as Woolwich Arsenal?

A. 1893

B. 1897

C. 1887

D. 1889

8. What was the name given to Arsenal FC when it was established?

A. Royal Arsenal

B. Woolwich Arsenal

C. Dial Square

D. The Arsenal

9. What team did Arsenal take on in their debut Premier League match?

A. Newcastle

B. Middlesbrough

C. Fulham

D. Norwich City

10. What year was the very first Arsenal Crest revealed?

A. 1883

B. 1888

C. 1892

D. 1898

11. What was the sum that each one of the 15 employees from Woolwich contributed to the club?

A. Six pence

B. Nine pence

C. Twelve pence

D. Fifteen pence

12. What's the philosophy that is the motto of Arsenal FC?

A. Null Satis Nisi the best (Nothing less than the very top is sufficient)

B. Mes Que un club (More than an club)

C. Consectatio Excellentiae (In the pursuit of excellence)

D. Victoria Concordia Crescit (Victory through harmony)

13. What was the country of the Arsenal FC's very first captain?

A. Swiss

B. Irish

C. English

D. Scottish

14. The year 1919 was the time that Arsenal were voted in the division of first division the cost of what club?

A. Chelsea

B. Tottenham Hotspur

C. Liverpool

D. Fulham

15. The mascot of the club is the symbol of which animal?

A. Lion

B. Bull

C. Dinosaur

D. Elephant

16. The very first English League match to be broadcast on radio live in 1927, was the match between Arsenal and what Club?

A. Sheffield United

B. Liverpool

C. Sheffield Wednesday

D. Manchester United

17. What was the first competition award attained by your club?

A. League Cup

B. FA Cup

C. First Division title

D. FA Charity Shield (FA Community Shield)

18. Which year was the year that Arsenal get their very first European trophy?

A. 1973

B. 1972

C. 1971

D. 1970

19. Who also contributed three shillings towards the formation of the club?

A. Henry Norris

B. David Danskin

C. Leslie Knighton

D. Morris Bates

20. Who was the Arsenal's first permanent manager?

A. Thomas Mitchell

B. William Elcoat

C. Harry Bradshaw

D. Leslie Knighton

20 Trivia Answers

1. C - 1904

2. B - 1913

3. B - 1886

4. D - The Gunners

5. C - David Danskin

6. B - 2002

7. A - 1893

8. C - Dial Square

9. D - Norwich City

10. B - 1888

11. A - Six Pence

12. D - Victoria Concordia Crescit (Victory Through Harmony)

13. D - Scotland

14. B - Tottenham Hotspur

15. C - Dinosaur

16. A - Sheffield United

17. B - FA Cup

18. D - 1970

19. B - David Danskin

20. A - Thomas Mitchell

10 Fun Facts

1. The Woolwich Arsenal Armament Factory employed a number of people. Woolwich Arsenal Armament Factory established the

club that is now called Arsenal FC in late 1886. At the time, the name began as Dial Square, in reference to the sundial located at the top of the main entrance into the factory.

2. In the wake of a 6-0 victory against Eastern Wanderers in their first-ever match on the 11th of December 1886, the term "Royal Arsenal" was chosen to replace the name 'Dial Square'. The name was derived from a mixture with the Royal Oak Pub, where the meeting of founders was held, as well as the place where they worked which was the Arsenal Armament Factory, located situated in Woolwich.

3. The iconic red colours of the club was adopted after the players who had recently taken on to Nottingham Forest asked their former club to borrow a kit. Arsenal kept the colours borrowed from other clubs.

Chapter 11: Stadium

20 Trivia Questions

1. What was the name given to the stadium that Arsenal used to play in, Highbury?

A. Home of Football

B. Stadium of Football

C. Home of the Gunners

D. Stadium of the Gunners

2. What club did Arsenal play against in their initial match that was played in the Emirates stadium?

A. Ajax

B. Portsmouth

C. Aston Villa

D. Benfica

3. What is the dimensions of the pitch for football on the pitch at Highbury Stadium?

A. 106 x 76 yards

B. 109 x 73 yards

C. 109 x 70 yards

D. 106 x 73 yards

4. Which was the very first Arsenal player to be issued a red card during the Emirates Stadium?

A. Philippe Senderos

B. Gilberto Silva

C. Lauren

D. Mathieu Flamini

5. What was the first architect to developed Highbury Stadium? Highbury Stadium?

A. Edwin Lutyens

B. Archibald Leitch

C. Herbert Baker

D. Populous

6. Which year was the Arsenal relocate to Highbury?

A. 1911

B. 1912

C. 1913

D. 1914

7. What is the location of the Emirates stadium situated?

A. Holloway

B. Harringay

C. Canonbury

D. Barnsbury

8. With what club Did Arsenal have the lowest attendance in Highbury during an League game?

A. Leeds United

B. Norwich City

C. Barnsley

D. Nottingham Forest

9. What's the pitch's size of the Emirates stadium?

A. 111.8 x 74.1 yards

B. 112.8 x 74.4 yards

C. 113.8 x 74.1 yards

D. 114.8 x 74.4 yards

10. How much was the price of the construction for Arsenal's present stadium?

A. PS350 million

B. PS390 million

C. PS450 million

D. PS590 million

11. Which was the very first footballer to be banned during the Emirates stadium?

A. Philippe Senderos

B. Sol Campbell

C. Ivan Campo

D. Rio Ferdinand

12. The stand in which stand of the Emirates stadium was once was known as The Laundry End?

A. North Bank Stand

B. South Stand

C. East Stand

D. West Stand

13. Which of these stadiums did Arsenal not use for a home field?

A. Field Mill

B. Invicta Ground

C. Manor Ground

D. Wembley Stadium

14. How big is the capacity in Emirates stadium? Emirates stadium?

A. 50,260

B. 55,260

C. 60,260

D. 65,260

15. Which architect firm designed The Emirates Stadium?

A. HMC Architects

B. Populous

C. Jacobs

D. LMN Architects

16. Which was the very first striker to score during a match that was competitive on the Emirates stadium?

A. Gabriel Agbonlahor

B. Gareth Barry

C. John Carew

D. Olof Mellberg

17. What was the very first Arsenal player to score a goal during an official match in the Emirates stadium?

A. Thierry Henry

B. Dennis Bergkamp

C. Gilberto Silva

D. Emmanuel Adebayor

18. What stand at The Emirates stadium is referred to for its nickname, the Clock End?

A. North Bank

B. East Stand

C. South Stand

D. West Stand

19. What was the biggest Arsenal winning margin of victory at Highbury?

A. 13:0

B. 11:0

C. 11:1

D. 13:1

20. Which Arsenal team was the opponent in the game that saw the largest attendance ever at Emirates stadium?

A. Manchester United

B. Tottenham Hotspur

C. Chelsea

D. Liverpool

20 Trivia Answers

1. A - Home of Football

2. C - Aston Villa

3. B - 109 x 73 yards

4. A - Philippe Senderos

5. B - Archibald Leitch

6. C - 1913

7. A - Holloway

8. A - Leeds United

9. D - 114.8 x 74.4 yards

10. B - PS390 Million

11. C - Ivan Campo

12. A - North Bank Stand

13. A - Field Mill

14. C - 60,250

15. B - Populous

16. D - Olof Mellberg

17. C - Gilberto Silva

18. C - South Stand

19. C - 11:1

20. A - Manchester United

10 Fun Facts

1. The early years of Arsenal moved between a variety of ground types in the Plumstead region. Royal Arsenal secured the lease of the Sportsman Ground on Plumstead Marshes after having played on Plumstead Common in their maiden season. The club soon moved to the Manor Ground due to increased attendance and the support of their fans.

2. The club relocated to the Invicta Stadium in the year 1891. The club remained there for almost six years, until an rise prompted them to move to their original Manor Ground home, which they purchased immediately. They remained on Manor Ground until their move to Highbury in 1913.

3. The last time Arsenal played at their old Manor Ground home was a 1-1 draw with Middlesbrough on the 26th of April 1913. The first game played match played at Highbury was a victory of 2-1 in the match against Leicester Fosse.

4. The Arsenal Stadium at Highbury was constructed through Archibald Leitch,

renowned for creating stands for teams such as Manchester United, Chelsea, Everton, Tottenham, and Glasgow Rangers. The stadium's main stand was on the east side, with a the capacity of 9,000 people.

5. The club made a payment of PS64,000 to get full ownership of the Highbury stadium. Restrictions such as the ban on playing during Christmas Day and Good Friday were eliminated.

Chapter 12: Managers

20 Trivia Questions

1. Who is the manager with the longest tenure at Arsenal?

A. Herbert Chapman

B. Arsene Wenger

C. George Graham

D. Bertie Mee

2. Who was the first Arsenal professional manager?

A. William Elcoat

B. Phil Kelso

C. George Morrell

D. Thomas Mitchell

3. Who was the manager who led Arsenal to the FA Cup in 1930?

A. George Graham

B. Tom Whittaker

C. Herbert Chapman

D. Jack Clayton

4. Which manager have won the European Cup Winners' Cup in the club?

A. George Graham

B. Arsene Wenger

C. Unai Emery

D. Terry Neill

5. Which one of these Arsenal managers have won many FA Cups for the club?

A. Arsene Wenger

B. George Graham

C. Herbert Chapman

D. Bertie Mee

6. What is Arsenal's 2nd longest-running manager?

A. Terry Neill

B. Bertie Mee

C. Tom Whittaker

D. George Allison

7. Which one of these managers succeeded George Graham in 1995?

A. Arsene Wenger

B. Bruce Rioch

C. Don Howe

D. Billy Wright

8. What is the citizenship of the former Arsenal director of football Unai Emery?

A. Danish

B. Swedish

C. French

D. Spanish

9. Which manager is represented by a statue in front of the Emirates stadium?

A. Herbert Chapman

B. Bertie Mee

C. George Graham

D. Terry Neill

10. Which one of them was for two distinct periods as caretaker managers?

A. Tom Whittaker

B. Stewart Houston

C. William Elcoat

D. Harry Bradshaw

11. Who was Arsenal's manager at the time that professional football returned in 1919?

A. James McEwen

B. Herbert Chapman

C. Leslie Knighton

D. Billy Wright

12. Who was the permanent manager who replaced Herbert Chapman after his unfortunate passing?

A. George Allison

B. Tom Whittaker

C. Jack Clayton

D. George Swindin

13. Which one of these Arsenal manager was previously as the physiotherapist at Arsenal?

A. George Swindin

B. Terry Neill

C. Steve Burtenshaw

D. Burtie Mee

14. Which of these managers wasn't an interim manager?

A. James McEwen

B. Joe Shaw

C. Bruce Rioch

D. Pat Rice

15. What the year of Arsene Wenger sworn in as Arsenal manager?

A. 1995

B. 1996

C. 1997

D. 1998

16. Which was the very first Arsenal manager to come from Scotland?

A. George Graham

B. George Morrell

C. Thomas Mitchell

D. Phil Kelso

17. Which manager didn't win the FA Cup for the club?

A. Unai Emery

B. Mikel Arteta

C. George Graham

D. Terry Neill

18. Was who the interim manager after Unai Emery departed the club?

A. Mikel Arteta

B. Dennis Bergkamp

C. Per Mertesacker

D. Freddie Ljungberg

19. Who was the first manager who wasn't English for Arsenal FC?

A. Unai Emery

B. Steve Burtenshaw

C. Arsene Wenger

D. Phil Kelso

20. Which manager has been the first to achieve an 'double' with Arsenal?

A. Bertie Mee

B. Arsene Wenger

C. George Graham

D. George Swindin

20 Trivia Answers

1. B - Arsene Wenger

2. D - Thomas Mitchell

3. C - Herbert Chapman

4. A - George Graham

5. A - Arsene Wenger

6. D - George Allison

7. B - Bruce Rioch

8. D - Spain

9. A - Herbert Chapman

10. B - Stewart Houston

11. C - Leslie Knighton

12. A - George Allison

13. D - Burtie Mee

14. C - Bruce Rioch

15. B - 1996

16. C - Thomas Mitchell

17. A - Unai Emery

18. D - Freddie Ljungberg

19. C - Arsene Wenger

20. A - Bertie Mee

10 Fun Facts

1. Sam Hollis was the first person in the team's affairs into his own hands after he was named Secretary-Manager in 1894. The club was managed by a group of players as well as club members prior to the appointment. He managed to keep the club on the top of the

table in the Second Division during his three years with the club until he was transferred to Bristol City in 1897.

2. Thomas Brown Mitchell was the first manager of professional status in Arsenal history, when he signed with the club in 1897. The Scotsman was the secretary of Blackburn Rovers for twelve years prior to being appointed manager. He guided Arsenal through the FA Cup qualifying rounds and sixth within the Second Division before resigning in March of 1898.

3. Harry Bradshaw is regarded as the Arsenal's most successful manager who led the club up to promotion into the First Division in 1904 and an impressive third place finish in the league between 1902 and 2003. Bradshaw was appointed manager of Fulham in the month of May 1904, and later was appointed Secretary of the Southern League.

4. Scotsman Phil Kelso was the first manager to lead Arsenal within the English premier league, having taken over the role from

promotion-winning coach Harry Bradshaw in 1904. The manager led the club to two FA Cup semifinals before leaving in 1908.

5. Woolwich Arsenal made the move from Plumstead in the southeast of London and then to Highbury within North London under the tutelage of George Morrell. Morrell took charge in 1908 and was ranked 6th in his debut season despite having to trade some of his most talented players. The club was the only one to be relegated to the second tier under his leadership, and finished at the bottom of the table in 1913.

Chapter 13: Goalies

20 Trivia Questions

1. Which one of the goalies have the most appearances at Arsenal FC?

A. David Seaman

B. Jens Lehman

C. Petr Cech

D. Manuel Almunia

2. Which club Did Jens Lehmann come to Arsenal F.C?

A. Stuttgart

B. Bayern Munich

C. Borussia Dortmund

D. Borussia Monchengladbach

3. Which one of these Arsenal goalkeepers who saved Paul Scholes' penalty in the 2005 FA Cup final?

A. Manuel Almunia

B. Jens Lehmann

C. Stuart Taylor

D. Vito Mannone

4. Which one of them was in the middle of the stick during the time the club was awarded the 2021 FA Cup?

A. Bernd Leno

B. David Ospina

C. Petr Cech

D. Emiliano Martinez

5. What of the Arsenal goalkeepers have took home the Premier League Golden Glove award?

A. Jens Lehmann

B. Wojciech Szczesny

C. David Seaman

D. Bernd Leno

6. Which goalie were in between the sticks during the time that the club was victorious in the 2017 FA Cup?

A. Petr Cech

B. Emiliano Martinez

C. Bernd Leno

D. David Ospina

7. What is the citizenship of the former Arsenal shooter Lukasz Fabianski?

A. Serbian

B. Croat

C. Polish

D. Albanian

8. How many clear sheets did Jens Lehmann manage to keep during 2005/06's Champions League campaign?

A. 8

B. 6

C. 4

D. 2

9. Which club did Aaron Ramsdale signed from?

A. Brighton & Hove Albion F.C

B. AFC Bournemouth

C. Sheffield United

D. Fulham F.C.

10. From where was Bernd Leno signed from?

A. Bayer Leverkusen

B. Vfb Stuttgart

C. Werder Bremen

D. Borussia Dortmund

11. Which Premier League appearances did John Lukic get for his second time at Arsenal?

A. 24

B. 21

C. 18

D. 15

12. The former Arsenal goalie Vito Mannone is from what country?

A. Spain

B. Italy

C. Netherlands

D. France

13. What number of FA Cups did David Seaman get during his time at Arsenal?

A. 6

B. 5

C. 4

D. 3

14. Which one of these goalies have scored a league goal on behalf of the club?

A. Frank Moss

B. David Seaman

C. George Swindin

D. Bob Wilson

15. What did Jens Lehmann's name mean to him?

A. Savior Jens

B. Great Jens

C. Brick Jens

D. Mad Jens

16. What's the nationality of the former Arsenal goalie Alfred Jack Kelsey?

A. English

B. Irish

C. Welsh

D. Scottish

17. Which goalies have Arsenal choose to sign with their arch-rivals Tottenham?

A. Pat Jennings

B. David Seaman

C. George Swindin

D. John Lukic

18. Which Arsenal goalkeeper is the club's record holder in clean sheets the most for the club?

A. Jens Lehmann

B. Petr Cech

C. John Lukic

D. David Seaman

19. What number of Premier League appearances did Vince Bartram make to the club?

A. 15

B. 11

C. 9

D. 7

20. Which among these Arsenal goalies lasted only twelve months at the club?

A. Richard Wright

B. Vito Mannone

C. Stuart Taylor

D. Alex Manninger

20 Trivia Answers

1. A - David Seaman

2. C - Borussia Dortmund

3. B - Jens Lehmann

4. D - Emiliano Martinez

5. B - Wojciech Szczesny

6. D - David Ospina

7. C - Poland

8. A - 8

9. C - Sheffield United

10. A - Bayer Leverkusen

11. C - 18

12. B - Italy

13. C - 4

14. A - Frank Moss

15. D - Mad Jens

16. C - Wales

17. A - Pat Jennings

18. D - David Seaman

19. B - 11

20. A - Richard Wright

10 Fun Facts

1. David Danskin is the first goalkeeper to be a part of Arsenal history to join the club the first season in Nottingham Forest. Because of him, and some others Nottingham Forest players

joining Arsenal during that time that year, the club was given its first dark red color scheme.

2. Arsenal have signed English goalkeeper Frank Moss, from Oldham Athletic for PS3,000 in the month of November 1931. The goalkeeper made his debut of his 143 appearances next day, at Chelsea. The player had a pretty prosperous time at the club with three league titles, as well as winning the Charity Shield a couple of occasions. He also made a league-winning goal during his time in the club.

3. For the majority of 2003/04, Jens Lehmann was in the goal as Arsenal triumphed to their third Premier League crown without suffering any defeat. The German had been signed by the club during the summer of 2003, after a move from Borussia Dortmund. He took home the FA Cup in 2005 and played a role in helping Arsenal get to the first UEFA Champions League final in 2006. He was also giving instructions to the players in the finale

in which Arsenal were defeated 2-1 by FC Barcelona.

4. Welshman, Jack Kelsey, was the first player to break into the Welsh team after sustaining injuries to Arsenal number one player, George Swindin. Jack played 29 games as Arsenal claimed the league championship in the same season. Jack was able to claim the first position in the league one year later. He was the representative of Wales during its initial World Cup appearance in 1958.

5. Over a career in the international arena which lasted for 22 years Pat Jennings made a record of 119 international appearances for Northern Ireland. He was a part of the team for eight years with Arsenal after having played thirteen years with Tottenham Hotspur. He played a key role in helping Arsenal get their first League as well as FA Cup double, and he's considered to be to be one of the greatest players of his position.

6. David Seaman is arguably the most effective Arsenal goalie of all time. The

Englishman had a record 564 appearances under the banner of Arsenal and was awarded nine important prizes which included League as well as FA Cup doubles in 1998 and 2002. He was instrumental in helping Arsenal win their 1994 UEFA Cup Winners Cup and played in the Gunners to an FA Cup victory in his final game of 2003.

7. John Lukic joined Arsenal for 75,000 pounds in July of 1983 to be an interim replacement for famous Pat Jennings. Lukic was the first choice of Arsenal's shot stopper after the halfway point of the 1984/85 campaign. He played a key role in helping the club achieve the League Cup in 1987 and the First Division title in 1989.

Chapter 14: Defenders

20 Trivia Questions

1. What number of Premier League title(s) did Ashley Cole win with Arsenal?

A. 1

B. 2

C. 3

D. 4

2. What did you think was Tony Adams' preferred position?

A. Left Back

B. Right Back

C. Centre Back

D. Wing Back

3. Which defender who won the European Cup Winners' Cup in the club?

A. Martin Keown

B. Nigel Winterburn

C. Pat Rice

D. Sol Campbell

4. What number of the FA Cup(s) have Tony Adams win with the club?

A. 4

B. 3

C. 2

D. 1

5. Which was Lee Dixon's favorite place of work?

A. Wing Back

B. Right Back

C. Left Back

D. Centre Back

6. Who was the Arsenal defender who received their 100th Premier League red card?

A. David Luiz

B. Rob Holding

C. Gabriel Magalhaes

D. Calum Chambers

7. Which of these heroes was not part of the 'Invincibles"?

A. Martin Keown

B. Kolo Toure

C. Pascal Cygan

D. Tony Adams

8. What is the country of the former Arsenal Left-back Gael Clichy?

A. French

B. English

C. Spanish

D. Italian

9. What defender is in the top spot for most games in the history of Arsenal?

A. Pat Rice

B. Nigel Winterburn

C. David O'Leary

D. Lee Dixon

10. Which defender is represented by a statue in the Emirates Stadium?

A. Nigel Winterburn

B. Tony Adams

C. Lee Dixon

D. Martin Keown

11. Where did Thomas Vermaelen signed?

A. Ajax F.C.

B. Club Brugge

C. Anderlecht

D. Feyenoord

12. Which of these players have not won a trophy in the club?

A. Bacary Sagna

B. Per Mertesacker

C. Kieran Gibbs

D. Johan Djourou

13. What number of League Cup(s) did David O'Leary win with the club?

A. 4

B. 3

C. 2

D. 1

14. Which of these defensive players was dubbed "Mr. Arsenal'?

A. Tony Adams

B. Martin Keown

C. David O'Leary

D. Sol Campbell

15. Which defender have not made at least 500 matches with the club?

A. Lee Dixon

B. Nigel Winterburn

C. Pat Rice

D. Martin Keown

16. What is the country of Arsenal the defender Pablo Mari?

A. Brazilian

B. Italian

C. Spanish

D. Ecuadorian

17. Which defender did not belong to the "famous four" Arsenal backline?

A. Steve Bould

B. Martin Keown

C. Tony Adams

D. Lee Dixon

18. Which club Was Lee Dixon signed?

A. Birmingham City

B. Chester City

C. Stoke City

D. Manchester City

19. Which one of the Arsenal defense players was not part of the FA Cup winning squad of 2019/20?

A. David Luiz

B. Callum Chambers

C. Cedric Soares

D. Laurent Koscielny

20. Who has the distinction of the player with the highest number of red cards Arsenal defense players from the Premier League?

A. Martin Keown

B. Laurent Koscielny

C. Tony Adams

D. David Luiz

20 Trivia Answers

1. B - 2

2. C - Centre Back

3. B - Nigel Winterburn

4. B - 3

5. B - Right Back

6. C - Gabriel Magalhaes

7. D - Tony Adams

Chapter 15: Midfielders

20 Trivia Questions

1. From where was Gilberto Silva signed from?

A. Atletico Madrid

B. Flamengo

C. Atletico Miniero

D. VfB Stuttgart

2. What number of Premier League title(s) did Robert Pires win at Arsenal F.C. ?

A. 4

B. 3

C. 2

D. 1

3. What was the number of assists Santi Cazorla record in his debut season at Arsenal F.C. ?

A. 16 aids

B. 14 assists

C. 12 helps

D. 10 assists

4. Which midfielder didn't win the team's 2005/2004 FA Cup?

A. Cesc Fabregas

B. Mathieu Flamini

C. Gilberto Silva

D. Abou Diaby

5. What trophy were they? Liam Brady win with the club?

A. First Division title

B. FA Cup

C. League Cup

D. FA Charity Cup (Community Shield)

6. Which among the ex- Arsenal midfielders hold the record in terms of "most red cards" among midfielders?

A. Gilberto Silva

B. Patrick Vieira

C. Alex Song

D. Francis Coquelin

7. What was the number of goals Robert Pires score in his debut season with Arsenal?

A. 10 goals

B. 8 goals

C. Six objectives

D. 4 goals

8. What was the place that Patrick Vieira signed from?

A. Monaco

B. Fiorentina

C. A.C Milan

D. Sporting CP

9. What number of assist did Mesut Ozil record during his first season with the club?

A. 17 aids

B. 15 assists

C. 13 helps

D. 11 assists

10. What is the country of origin for Arsenal midfielder Lucas Torreira?

A. Paraguay

B. Uruguay

C. Argentina

D. Bolivia

11. Which midfielder were the ones who returned to their club as coach?

A. Patrick Vieira

B. Dennis Bergkamp

C. Gilberto Silva

D. Mikel Arteta

12. Which midfielder have returned back to their club as technical directors?

A. Ian Wright

B. Eduardo Gaspar

C. Freddie Ljungberg

D. Ray Parlour

13. What number of FA Cups did Aaron Ramsey take home during his time at the club?

A. 5

B. 4

C. 3

D. 2

14. What was the time Mesut Ozil's journey to record the first Premier League assist?

A. 70 minutes

B. 41 minutes

C. 31.

D. 11 minutes

15. Which midfielder took home their first trophy in 1970, the European Fairs' Cup with Arsenal?

A. Peter Storey

B. Michael Thomas

C. David Jack

D. Anders Limpar

16. Which midfielder didn't make the team that won the title in 1990/91?

A. Michael Thomas

B. David Rocastle

C. Paul Davis

D. David Platt

17. Which one of these Arsenal midfielders earned the nickname 'The Romford Pele"?

A. David Rocastle

B. Ray Parlour

C. David Platt

D. Gilberto Silva

18. Which midfielder have not won a trophy in the club?

A. Denilson Neves

B. Jermaine Pennant

C. Eduardo Gasper

D. Ray Parlour

19. Which club has sold Granit Xhaka to Arsenal F.C. ?

A. Basel

B. Benfica

C. Borussia Monchengladbach

D. Borussia Dortmund

20. What Arsenal midfielder has been known as "The Little Mozart"?

A. Mesut Ozil

B. Santi Carzola

C. Cesc Fabregas

D. Tomas Rosicky

20 Trivia Answers

1. C - Atletico Mineiro

2. C - 2

3. B - 14 Assists

4. D - Abou Diaby

5. B - FA Cup

6. B - Patrick Vieira

7. A - 10 Goals

8. C - Milan

9. C - 13 Assists

10. B - Uruguay

11. D - Mikel Arteta

12. B - Eduardo Gasper

13. C - 3

14. D - 11 Minutes

15. A - Peter Storey

16. D - David Platt

17. B - Ray Parlour

18. A - Denilson Neves

19. C - Borussia Monchengladbach

20. D - Tomas Rosicky

10 Fun Facts 1. Patrick Vieira remains the last Arsenal captain who led the club to glory in the championship winning the title

undefeated in 2003/04. It is widely believed that he was the greatest midfielder of the club's past and was in the middle of nearly all the good things that the Gunners performed from 1996 until 2005. The last time he kicked, the club resulted in a 5-4 penalty shootout win against Manchester United in the 2005 FA Cup final.

2. French World Cup and European Championship winner, Robert Pires, regularly hit double figures for goals and assists during each of his impressive 6 years in Highbury. Robert Pires helped Arsenal achieve the two Premier League titles and three FA Cups, scoring the winner of a 1-1 FA Cup final win against Southampton in 2003.

3. Irish midfielder Liam Brady, had almost all the attributes a midfielder needs such as speed, agility ability, technique as well as strength and the ability to beat the opponent effortlessly. Brady was able to make his Arsenal debut in 1973, and played in the squad which reached three consecutive FA

Cup finals, winning the trophy with Manchester United in 1979. He was named PFA The Year's Player in 1979, and then left to join Juventus the following year.

4. Swedish midfielder Fredrik "Freddie" Ljungberg made a splash in his unforgettable Arsenal debut with an assist in the 3-1 win over title-chasing rivals Manchester United. In total, he scored 17 goals when the Gunners achieved their third League as well as FA Cup double in four years in the 2001/02 season. He was named the player of the year, and played an important role in the Gunners progress to winning their third Premier League crown a couple of years following.

Chapter 16: Forwards

20 Trivia Questions

1. Who was the greatest goal-scorer for Arsenal?

A. Theirry Henry

B. Ian Wright

C. Robin Van Persie

D. Dennis Bergkamp

2. How many games did it need to Thierry Henry to get his first goal at Arsenal?

A. 2

B. 4

C. 5

D. 7

3. Which club Was Ian Wright signed?

A. Greenwich

B. Celtic

C. Crystal Palace

D. Westham

4. What was the number of goals Nwankwo Kanu score for Arsenal?

A. 86

B. 56

C. 98

D. 44

5. What team did Arsenal score the first Champions League hat-trick against?

A. Inter Milan

B. FC Basel

C. Galatasaray

D. AS Roma

6. Which was the very first Arsenal striker to bag an Champions League Hattrick?

A. Nikolas Bendtner

B. Thierry Henry

C. Danny Welbeck

D. Oliver Giroud

7. What club Did Emmanuel Adebayo score his first goal in the club of Arsenal?

A. Manchester United

B. Sheffield United

C. Birmingham City

D. Sunderland

8. The last time he played for Arsenal What was the number of scores Did Robin Van Persie score?

A. 30

B. 35

C. 33

D. 32

9. What was the number of goals Oliver Giroud score for Arsenal?

A. 98

B. 105

C. 109

D. 110

10. Which were adversaries at the time Julio Baptista scored his first three-pointer for Arsenal?

A. Bolton Wanderers

B. Norwich City

C. Aston Villa

D. Liverpool

11. When he made his debut with Arsenal How many scores Did Ian Wright score?

A. 14

B. 19

C. 28

D. 24

12. Who did you score the winner against Manchester united in 2015's FA Cup Round 6?

A. Danny Welbeck

B. Aaron Ramsey

C. Oliver Giroud

D. Mesut Ozil

13. What club did Kanu quit Arsenal to join?

A. Portsmouth

B. Ajax

C. West Brom

D. Inter Milan

14. What was the number of goals Alexis Sanchez score in the 2016-2017 season?

A. 42

B. 30

C. 36

D. 29

15. What was the greatest goal scorer during the Invincibles season?

A. Theirry Henry

B. Dennis Bergkamp

C. Robert Pires

D. Nwankwo Kanu

16. Which among these French clubs bought the Emmanual Adebayor for Arsenal?

A. Lille

B. Rennes

C. Marseille

D. Monaco

17. What was the number of goals Eduardo scored in his time at Arsenal?

Chapter 17: Captains

20 Trivia Questions

1. What is the most-respected captain at Arsenal?

A. Pat Rice

B. Bill Julain

C. Laurent Koscielny

D. Tony Adams

2. Who was captain of the Invincibles season?

A. Tony Adams

B. Patrick Viera

C. Thierry Henry

D. Dennis Bergkamp

3. Who was captain of Arsenal in 2006's Champions League final?

A. Robin Van Persie

B. Thierry Henry

C. Cesc Fabregas

D. Kolo Toure

4. Which was the very first captain to be awarded the League Cup for the club?

A. Kenny Samson

B. Pat Rice

C. Adam Bill

D. Tony Adams

5. Who was captain of 2001/2002's Premier League season?

A. Patrick Viera

B. Tony Adams

C. Billy Bates

D. Alf Baker

6. What is the youngest player ever to become a permanent captain of Arsenal?

A. Tony Adams

B. Cesc Fabregas

C. Robin Van Persie

D. Jack Wilshere

7. Who was the captain of Arsene Wenger's last home match?

A. Per Mertesacker

B. Granit Xhaka

C. Petr Cech

D. Laurent Koscielny

8. Who was the captain of Arsenal during the 2016-2017 FA Cup final?

A. Per Mertesacker

B. Laurent Koscielny

C. Mikel Arteta

D. Granit Xhaka

9. Who is currently the Captain of Arsenal?

A. Pierre-Emeric Aubameyang

B. Alexandre Lacazette

C. Granit Xhaka

D. Rob Holding

10. Which was the most recent player to be captain of Arsenal for the Champions League?

A. Per Mertesacker

B. Laurent Koscielny

C. Mikel Arteta

D. Granit Xhaka

11. Who was captain of Arsenal in the Baku Europa League final?

A. Mikel Arteta

B. Granit Xhaka

C. Laurent Koscielny

D. Per Mertesacker

12. Who was leader of the Arsenal team to take home their very first English Premier League?

A. Tony Adams

B. Steve Bould

C. Lee Dixon

D. Nigel Winterburn

13. Who was captain of Arsenal in the time they were first winners of the FA Cup?

A. Billy Blyth

B. Charlie Jones

C. Tom Parker

D. Charlie Buchan

14. Who was Captain for the Arsenal team which took home the inaugural FA Cup under Wenger?

A. Lee Dixon

B. Tony Adams

C. Steve Bould

D. Charlie Buchan

15. Which captains have did they win their Premier League and FA Cup two times while at Arsenal?

A. Patrick Viera

B. Tony Adams

C. Steve Bould

D. Frank McLintock

16. What was the very first Arsenal captain?

A. Arthur Brown

B. Bill Julian

C. David Danskin

D. Moris Bates

17. Which one of these Arsenal captains departed for Juventus?

A. Patrick Viera

B. Thierry Henry

C. Moris Bates

D. Charlie Buchan

18. What was the duration of Tony Adams' captaincy?

A. 1985-2002

B. 1989-2002

C. 1988-2002

D. 1990-2002

19. Who coached the FA Cup-winning team in 1998?

A. Patrick Viera

B. Tony Adams

C. Steve Bould

D. Charlie Buchan

20. Who was leader of the team who took home the inaugural Community Shield?

A. Billy Blyth

B. Tom Parker

C. Alex Barker

D. Alf Baker

20 Trivia Answers

1. D - Tony Adams

2. B - Patrick Viera

3. B - Thierry Henry

4. A - Kenny Samson

5. B - Tony Adams

6. A - Tony Adams

7. C - Petr Cech

8. A - Per Mertesacker

9. B - Alexandre Lacazette

10. B - Laurent Koscielny

11. C - Laurent Koscielny

12. A - Tony Adams

13. C - Tom Parker

14. B - Tony Adams

15. B - Tony Adams

16. C - David Danskin

17. A - Patrick Viera

18. C - 1988-2002

19. B - Tony Adams

20. B - Tom Parker

10 Fun Facts

1. The initial player who was captain of Arsenal Football Club was a goalkeeper known as David Danskin. David was the first founding member of the club and was a partially employed mechanical engineer.

2. Tony Adams is the club's longest-serving captain (14 years between 1988 and 2002). Adams is a player for one club that gave him

the nickname "MR Arsenal." He participated in 669 matches and was awarded 10 trophies.

3. Patrick Vieira succeeded Tony Adams and was captain of the club in its most productive period (2002 through 2005) during that Premier League era. Vieira also concluded his tenure at Arsenal with a bang with a winning penalty in the 2004/2005 FA cup championship against opponents, Manchester United. He finished his career with three EPL and five FA Cups, and 3 English supercups.

4. Following Vieira, Thierry Henry took his captain's armband. Arsenal made it to the UEFA Champions League final for the first time under his leadership. On an emotional evening that saw goalkeeper Jens Lehmann exiled, Arsenal lost 2-1 to Barcelona

5. The youngest captain of the gunners team is Terry Neill, who was just 20 years old and 102 months when he was appointed captain. His debut came with Sheffield Wednesday at eighteen years old, in December of 1960. He

was appointed captain a year later in the year 1962.

6. The 2nd-youngest person to be captain of Arsenal was Cesc Fabregas. He was the youngest to take his place at the age of 21 years old and the 204th day. Cesc Fabregas was the one to lead Arsenal to their return to Champions League football, including an appearance in the semi-finals of the 2008/09 season.

Chapter 18: Titles

20 Trivia Questions

1. What number of European distinctions do Arsenal are awarded?

A. 0

B. 1

C. 2

D. 3

2. How long has Arsenal not won the Premier League?

A. 19

B. 20

C. 18

D. 17

3. What number of Premier League titles have Arsenal taken home?

A. 3

B. 4

C. 5

D. 10

4. What number of League titles (in all) do Arsenal own?

A. 16

B. 15

C. 13

D. 12

5. What is the most recent time Arsenal taken home the FA Cup?

A. 12

B. 14

C. 15

D. 11

6. Which Community Shields have Arsenal won?

A. 12

B. 5

C. 19

D. 16

7. What team Did Arsenal take home her 10-time FA Cup final?

A. Chelsea

B. Westham United

C. Manchester United

D. Liverpool

8. What was the final score in the thirteenth FA cup final?

A. 2-1

B. 3-0

C. 1-1

D. 4-2

9. What was the biggest Arsenal victory in an FA Cup final?

A. 3-2

B. 4-1

C. 5-2

D. 4-0

10. What is the most FA Cup and League double did Arsenal been able to win?

A. 1

B. 2

C. 4

D. 3

11. Which trophies have Arsenal taken home during the Emirate Stadium era?

A. 2

B. 4

C. 6

D. 8

12. What was the most recent trophy taken home in Highbury Stadium? Highbury Stadium?

A. The FA Cup

B. The Premier League

C. The Carling Cup

D. The Champions League

13. What was the very first significant trophy that was awarded in the Emirates?

A. The Carling Cup

B. The FA Cup

C. The Community Shield

D. The Premier League

14. In which team against which team did Arsenal have their greatest FA Cup final win?

A. Hull City

B. Manchester United

C. Aston Villa

D. Chelsea

15. How many times has Arsenal been a FA Cup final runner-up?

A. 10

B. 7

C. 8

D. 9

16. What was the final score of the team's eleventh FA Cup final win?

A. 3:2

B. 2:1

C. 3:0

D. 1:0

17. What is the most recent time that Arsenal been able to win two consecutive FA Cups?

A. 4

B. 3

C. 2

D. 1

18. What is the most recent time Arsenal been able to win two consecutive League title?

A. 2

B. 3

C. 1

D. 4

19. How many league titles has Arsenal taken home?

A. 4

B. 3

C. 2

D. 1

20. What number of back-to-back Community Shield titles has Arsenal been awarded?

A. 1

B. 2

C. 3

D. 4

20 Trivia Answers

1. C - 2

2. D - 17

3. A - 3

4. C - 13

5. B - 14

6. D - 16

7. C - Manchester United

8. A - 2:1

9. D - 4:0

10. D - 3

11. D - 8

12. A - The FA Cup

13. B - FA Cup

14. C - Aston Villa

15. B - 7

16. A - 3:2

17. C - 2

18. A - 2

19. B - 3

20. C - 3

10 Fun Facts

1. The club has won 14 times. Arsenal FC are the kings of the FA cup. They took it home first time back in 1930, and their last win came in the year 2020.

2. The first award the club ever took home was the Kent Junior Cup, won by the reserve team. The first team did not let them down. Three weeks later they won Kent seniors cup. Kent seniors ' cup.

3. Arsenal FC has accomplished the Cup and league double three times. The club achieved this feat in the 1970/71, 1997/98 and 2001/02 seasons. Arsenal still hasn't managed to achieve more impressive feat of the domestic triple. But, they also achieved their FA as well as the League Cup double in 1992/93.

Chapter 19: Memorable Games

20 Trivia Questions

1. Which were their initial players to play at the brand new Emirates stadium?

A. Ajax

B. Aston Villa

C. Westham

D. Stoke City

2. What is the biggest crowd count in Emirate Stadium? Emirate stadium?

A. 59,232

B. 60,161

C. 61,543

D. 58,765

3. What was the result of the most devastating defeat for Arsenal within the Premier League?

A. 8:2

B. 6:0

C. 7:1

D. 8:0

4. Was the scoring line for the biggest Arsenal win of the Champions League?

A. 6:0

B. 8:0

C. 7:0

D. 11:2

5. Which one of these footballers have admitted to throwing the pizza towards Sir Alex Ferguson of Manchester United in the notorious Pizzagate scandal?

A. Patrick Vieira

B. Kolo Toure

C. Cesc Fabregas

D. Robert Pires

6. What was the final scoreline of Arsenal's greatest victory in the FA Cup?

A. 12:0

B. 11:1

C. 10:2

D. 13:0

7. Who were your last team to face in Highbury stadium? Highbury stadium?

A. Derby County

B. Wigan Athletic

C. Bolton Wanderers

D. Stoke City

8. Which side handed Arsenal the biggest loss of their club during the FA Cup?

A. Bolton Athletic

B. Sunderland

C. Liverpool

D. Derby County

9. What was the result of the top-scoring North London rivalry between Arsenal as well as Tottenham Hotspurs?

A. 4:3

B. 6:0

C. 5:4

D. 4:4

10. Arsenal beat Spurs during the September 2021 match on the Emirates. Which was the final score?

A. 3:1

B. 3:0

C. 1:0

D. 4:0

11. What team has ended Arsenal's record-breaking of 49 consecutive matches without losing?

A. Chelsea

B. Manchester United

C. Sunderland

D. Manchester City

12. What team did Arsenal get their start on their 49-game in a winless Premier League run against?

A. Wigan Athletic

B. Southampton

C. Sunderland

D. Middlesbrough

13. Which were UCL opposition at the time Arsenal had 11 players of various nationalities in the year the year 2006?

A. Hamburg S.V

B. Borussia Dortmund

C. Valencia C.F

D. Liverpool F.C

14. On the 14th of February in 2005, Arsenal had an all-foreign team of players. Who were the opposition?

A. Leeds United

B. Southampton F.C

C. Crystal Palace

D. West Bromwich Albion

15. What team did Arsenal take part in their very initial Champions League match against?

A. RC Lens

B. Inter Milan

C. Standard Liege

D. Lyon

16. Arsenal had to come back from defeat in order in order to take this 2013/14 FA Cup final. Was the score of the first game?

A. 2:0

B. 3:0

C. 1:0

D. 4:0

17. Which Arsenal player scored the opening goal during their comeback to 2013/14's FA Cup Final?

A. Alex Iwobi

B. Aaron Ramsey

C. Santi Cazorla

D. Laurent Koscielny

18. What was the final score of Arsenal's most important home victory against Tottenham Hotspurs during the PL time period?

A. 5:1

B. 4:2

C. 5:2

D. 6:2

19. What was the result of Arsenal's greatest away win against Chelsea?

A. 6:0

B. 5:1

C. 7:2

D. 5:0

20. What was the final score of Arsenal's most important away victory in the Premier League against Tottenham Hotspurs?

A. 5:2

B. 6:0

C. 4:3

D. 7:1

20 Trivia Answers

1. A - Ajax

2. B - 60,161

3. A - 8:2

4. C - 7:0

5. C - Cesc Fabregas

6. B - 11:1

7. B - Wigan Athletic

8. B - Sunderland

9. C - 5:4

10. A - 3:1

11. B - Manchester United

12. B - Southampton

13. A - Hamburg SV

14. C - Crystal Palace

15. A - RC Lens

16. A - 2:0

17. C - Santi Cazorla

18. C - 5:2

19. B - 5:1

20. B - 6:0

10 Fun Facts

1. Nowadays, Arsenal is the king of the English FA Cup, but they started with a team. This was the 1929/30 season, when they won an 2-0 win against Huddersfield Town. The first significant award isn't all which makes this game important to Arsenal supporters and everyone else who is a lover of the game. It was the first game in which was broadcast by the BBC had ever afforded broadcasting rights. It is also an early start for the lucrative TV rights of the league.

2. The sport of football has plenty of exciting competitions to be thrilling, however only a handful are truly amazing that fans of teams that lose cheer and praise the winners. The 1970-71 season saw Arsenal won 2-1 against Liverpool by a score of 2-1 during the semi-final of the FA Cup to cement their first ever domestic (league/cup) dual. The team came from behind scoring two goals in the final minutes and the match-winner, Charlie

George, gave us the famous "lying down on my back" celebration.

3. In 2013, following nine years without winning a trophy Arsenal won their first FA cup by putting Hull City to a 3-2 loss. Hull City were the underdogs but the final wasn't a easy win. Within 10 minutes of the start of the game at half-time, Hull City were a goal down. Gunners had been beaten by two goals. They came back with Santi Cazorla. They also scored a goal through Laurent Koscielny, and then sent the match into overtime which is when Aaron Ramsey popped up 11 minutes before the final whistle to secure the win.

www.ingramcontent.com/pod-product-compliance
Lightning Source LLC
Chambersburg PA
CBHW071439080526
44587CB00014B/1916